HORRIBLE HISTORIES

EGYPT

A HIGH-SPEED HISTORY

SNAP!

TERRY DEARY

ILLUSTRATED BY

DAVE SMITH

SCHOLASTIC

For Cat Clarke, with thanks. TD

For Rachel, no. 1 mummy. DS

SCHOLASTIC CHILDREN'S BOOKS,
EUSTON HOUSE, 24 EVERSHOLT STREET,
LONDON NW1 1DB, UK

A DIVISION OF SCHOLASTIC LTD
LONDON ~ NEW YORK ~ TORONTO ~ SYDNEY ~ AUCKLAND
MEXICO CITY ~ NEW DELHI ~ HONG KONG

PUBLISHED IN THE UK BY SCHOLASTIC LTD, 2010

TEXT COPYRIGHT © TERRY DEARY, 2010
ILLUSTRATIONS COPYRIGHT © DAVE SMITH, 2010

ALL RIGHTS RESERVED

ISBN 978 1407 111865

PRINTED AND BOUND BY TIEN WAH PRESS PTE. LTD, SINGAPORE

24681097531

CONTENTS

Three thousand years is a very long time. Even your history teacher isn't that old... Most history teachers retire when they are 300 years old. (Well, mine did.)

Ancient Egypt went on for about 3000 years and your history books can't tell you everything that happened in that time. They can just pick the important bits.

THE BITS YOU REALLY WANT TO KNOW ARE THE HORRIBLE AND THE GRUESOME BITS.

PLEASE, SIR, WHAT DID THE EGYPTIANS DO TO YOU IF THEY CAUGHT YOU ROBBING A TOMB?

THEY NAILED YOU TO THE WALLS OF THE CITY ... BUT THAT IS NOT IN THE EXAM SO FORGET IT

THERE'S THE PROBLEM.

I WANT A HIGH-SPEED HISTORY...

BUT WE ALSO WANT A 'HORRIBLE' HISTORY

ANYONE WILL TELL YOU...

YOU CAN'T HAVE A HIGH-SPEED HORRIBLE HISTORY

WELL, YOU CAN NOW. AND HERE IT IS. JUST THE BEST STORIES FROM EGYPT'S HISTORY ... BECAUSE YOU HAVEN'T GOT A SPARE 3000 YEARS. AND JUST THE HORRIBLY INTERESTING BITS THAT TEACHER NEVER TELLS YOU.

SIR ... HOW DID QUEEN CLEOPATRA DIE HORRIBLY?

SHE WAS BITTEN BY A SNAKE

WRONG ANSWER!

OH DEAR! BETTER LEND ME THAT BOOK

HORRIBLE HEALTH WARNING!

THIS BOOK IS NOT SUITABLE FOR TEACHERS!!!

HANDS OFF!!

OSIRIS
AND THE FIRST
MUMMY 3500 BC

EGYPT IS FAMOUS FOR TURNING ITS KINGS AND QUEENS INTO MUMMIES. THAT'S A BIT ODD. NO ONE IS THINKING OF TURNING YOUR QUEEN INTO A MUMMY – NOT EVEN WHEN SHE'S DEAD. SO WHERE ON EARTH DID THE EGYPTIANS GET THIS ODD IDEA? IT ALL STARTED WITH A GRUESOME EGYPTIAN LEGEND.

LET'S START WITH THE GODDESS ISIS ... THE GODDESS OF THE SIMPLE.

WATCH WHO YOU'RE CALLING SIMPLE!

SET PLAYED A CRUEL TRICK. HE SAID...

I HAVE THE WORLD'S FINEST WOOD COFFIN. WHOEVER FITS INTO IT CAN HAVE IT!

YOU'RE A PET, SET

YOU BET

NO ONE FITTED THE STONE COFFIN. NOT ISIS...

I'M UPSET, SET

I REGRET

...UNTIL OSIRIS TRIED IT.

PERFECT

OSIRIS LAY BACK. THAT'S WHEN SNEAKY SET SLAMMED THE LID AND SEALED THE COFFIN.

I'LL RUN TO THE NILE WHILE I SMILE ... SMILE, SMILE, SMILE

SET THREW IT IN. THE COFFIN FLOATED MILES ON THE NILE BUT GOT STUCK IN A TREE TRUNK. A QUEEN SAID...

CUT DOWN THIS TRUNK AND USE IT TO BUILD MY PALACE AT BYBLOS

ALAS! I'VE TWO BROTHERS. ONE'S A KILLER ... THE OTHER'S A PILLAR!

ISIS RESCUED HIS BODY WITHOUT THE PALACE FALLING DOWN.

I WASN'T A KEEN QUEEN, BUT IT WORKED!

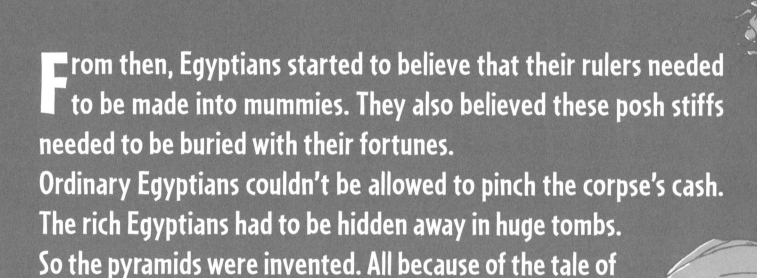

From then, Egyptians started to believe that their rulers needed to be made into mummies. They also believed these posh stiffs needed to be buried with their fortunes.

Ordinary Egyptians couldn't be allowed to pinch the corpse's cash. The rich Egyptians had to be hidden away in huge tombs. So the pyramids were invented. All because of the tale of Isis and Osiris.

POWER OF THE PYRAMIDS

Around 2560 BC

A DEAD OLD KING WOULD NEED LOTS OF MONEY IN THE AFTERLIFE. SO HE WAS BURIED WITH TREASURES. AND ROBBERS SOON LEARNED TO LOOT THE TOMBS. THE EGYPTIANS NEEDED TO BUILD BIGGER AND BIGGER PYRAMIDS TO KEEP THEM OUT.

THE PYRAMIDS TOOK SO LONG TO BUILD THEY HAD TO START WORK WHILE THE PHARAOH (OR KING) WAS STILL ALIVE.

NOW, HEMON, I EXPECT TO DIE IN ABOUT 10 YEARS' TIME. BUILD ME A PYRAMID. THE BIGGEST THE WORLD HAS EVER SEEN

YES, LORD KHUFU

THEY START WITH A BARE STRETCH OF DESERT ROCK...

OOOOH! I'LL GET A WET COFFIN, HEMON!

FIRST WE LET WATER FROM THE NILE FLOOD THE ROCK...

NO, HIGHNESS KHUFU. WATER IS FLAT... WE USE IT TO CHECK THE BASE IS FLAT

CLE-VER. I DON'T WANT A PYRAMID WITH A TILTED TOP, DO I?

WE START WITH FOUR SIDES FACING EXACTLY NORTH, SOUTH, EAST AND WEST

DON'T TELL ME ... LET ME GUESS ... YOU USE THE POLE STAR TO WORK OUT WHERE THE NORTH IS

YEARS PASS,
AS MONTHS DO ...
ONLY TWELVE TIMES LONGER...

WE ADD NEW LEVELS – EACH ONE SMALLER THAN THE ONE BEFORE

LET'S MAKE SURE THERE'S A REAL POINT TO THIS BUILDING. HA! HA! THAT'S A JOKE, YOU KNOW

19

22

AT LAST THE PYRAMID WAS FINISHED. IT WAS COVERED IN SMOOTH, WHITE STONE.

HUFU DIED AND WAS TURNED INTO A MUMMY. HE WAS BURIED IN THE KING'S CHAMBER ... MAYBE. IN AD 820 - THOUSANDS OF YEARS LATER - AN ARAB KING ENTERED THE PYRAMID AND FOUND...

HUGE BLOCKS OF STONE FILLED THE PASSAGEWAY. THIEVES HAD NOT BROKEN IN, YET THE COFFIN WAS EMPTY AND...

NOTHING!

THIS COFFIN IS TOO SMALL TO HOLD A CORPSE ANYWAY ... UNLESS THE LEGS ARE BENT

AND WHERE ARE THE PHARAOH'S TREASURES?

IT'S A HISTORY MYSTERY. WHAT HAPPENED TO KHUFU AND HIS TREASURE?

THE TOMB WAS PROBABLY ROBBED BY THE ANCIENT EGYPTIANS. BUT MANY PYRAMIDS WERE ROBBED BY THE VERY PEOPLE WHO WERE SUPPOSED TO GUARD THEM.

WOULD I DO SUCH A THING? HEH! HEH!

Tomb builders, guards and priests could all help with a robbery. Promise to give them a share of the loot and they will let you rob the grave and get away. In the end the Egyptians saw that pyramids didn't work. They started burying their kings in tombs dug into the rock – a new graveyard called 'The Valley of the Kings'.

In AD 1301 an earthquake shook all the bright white stones off the Great Pyramid of Khufu. The pyramid you can see today is not the smooth and gleaming tomb that Khufu had built.

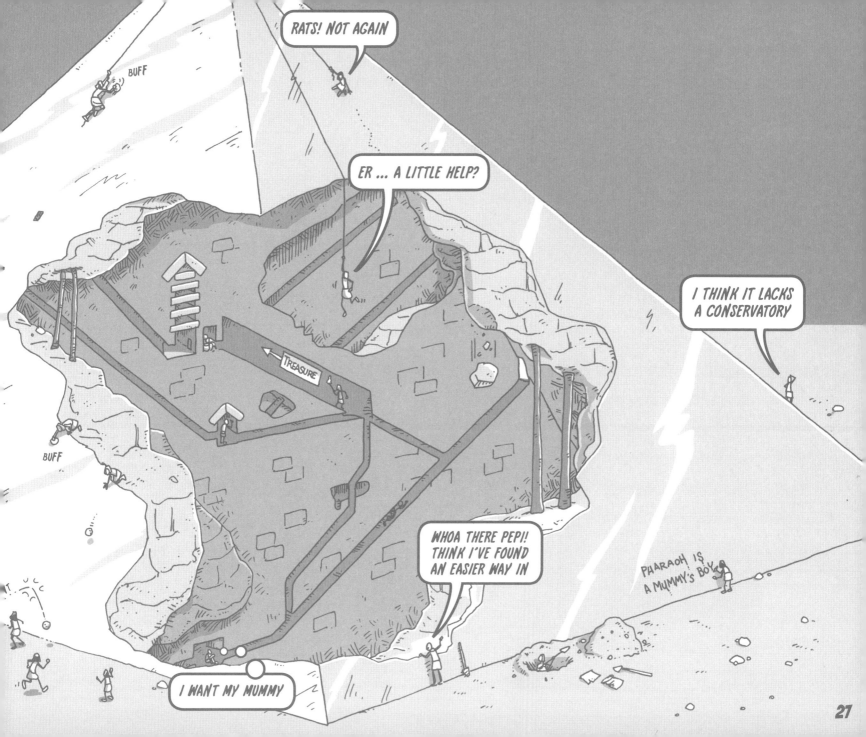

27

BANDAGES
AND
BRAINS

AROUND 2000 BC

BODIES ROT IN THE HOT EGYPTIAN SUN. THE EGYPTIANS NEEDED TO FIND A WAY TO STOP THE ROT. AFTER A FEW ROTTEN EXPERIMENTS THEY BECAME QUITE GOOD AT MAKING MUMMIES ... BUT IT WASN'T A JOB FOR PEOPLE WHO ARE SICK AT THE SIGHT OF A SQUASHED HEDGEHOG.

31

34

It took the ancient Egyptians about 1500 years to get mummy-making right. The first mummies were just wrapped in bandages and left to rot. When their coffins were opened they smelled terrible. But Egyptian COOKS taught the mummy-makers the best way to keep meat fresh was to gut an animal and keep its body in salt. Yummy mummy.

THE PHUNNIEST PHARAOH

AROUND **1490** BC

SOME PHARAOHS CAME AND WENT AND HISTORY HARDLY NOTICED. BUT SOME REALLY, **REALLY** MADE A DIFFERENCE TO EGYPT. PHARAOHS LIKE HATSHEPSUT.

HATSHEPSUT WAS A PRINCESS OF EGYPT, AND SENENMUT WAS HER DAUGHTER'S TEACHER.

HATSHEPSUT IS AN AMAZING WOMAN ... STRANGE, BUT AMAZING

I LIKE TO THINK OF MYSELF AS A SUPER-WOMAN SEN, ME OLD LAD!

SHE HAS GRAND IDEAS...

I COULD RULE THIS COUNTRY OF EGYPT, YOU KNOW. REALLY RULE IT

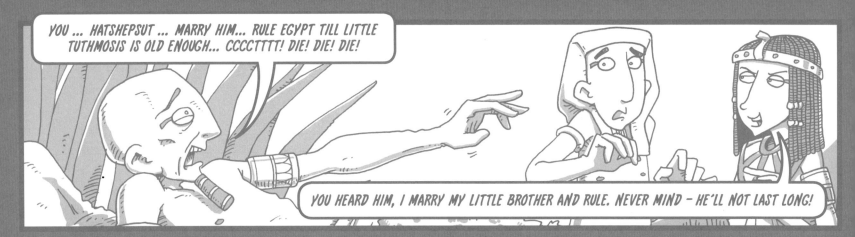

HANG ON! A PHARAOH HAS TO HAVE A BEARD!

HERE, SENENMUT ... WHY DIDN'T YOU THINK OF THAT?

I DID, MAJESTY – HERE'S ONE I MADE EARLIER

SO HATSHEPSUT WORE A **FALSE BEARD...**

I'VE EVEN HAD ALL YOUR STATUES AND CARVINGS MADE WITH A BEARD. A CHIN WIG

BETTER THAN AN EARWIG, I SUPPOSE...

CHINK CHINK CHOP

OF COURSE, YOUNG TUTHMOSIS **III** WAS A BIT PUT OUT WHEN HIS AUNTY HAT TOOK THE CROWN THAT SHOULD HAVE BEEN HIS.

I AM **VERY** PUT OUT

SOME PEOPLE SAY TUTHMOSIS HAD HER POISONED

SOME PEOPLE USE RAT POISON ... I USE HAT POISON... HEH! HEH!

AND TO MAKE IT WORSE SHE LIVED TO A GOOD OLD AGE

I'VE BEEN **VERY** PUT OUT FOR A **VERY** LONG TIME – 22 YEARS. MAYBE I SHOULD DO SOMETHING ABOUT IT!

Tuthmosis III's plot to make the world forget Hatshepsut didn't work. Her temple at Karnak on the Nile is still one of the greatest Egyptian tombs ... and people take MORE notice of her statues because Tuthmosis had them hacked about.

DJEHUTY FRUITY

AROUND 1500 BC

Tuthmosis III was a fighter. He led his Egyptian forces and invaded countries and faced great dangers. Once he had to be rescued from a herd of wild elephants. On another hunt (they say) he killed 120 elephants with his own sword – that's a jumbo task. But Tuthmosis III couldn't be everywhere. Sometimes he had to send his generals to do the fighting for him. Sneaky generals like Djehuty...

GENERAL DJEHUTY. THE PEOPLE OF JOPPA ARE REVOLTING. CAPTURE JOPPA AND PUNISH THEM

YES, BOSS. I'LL BE YOUR JOPPA CHOPPER

BUT BEFORE DJEHUTY LEFT, TUT **III** GAVE AN ORDER TO A SERVANT...

HIDE MY CANE OF POWER IN THE GENERAL'S LUGGAGE. IT WILL GIVE HIM MAGIC POWERS

SURE THING, KING

DJEHUTY ATTACKED THE WALLS OF JOPPA BUT WAS KNOCKED BACK...

DJEHUTY DRESSED AS A SERVANT AND VISITED THE JOPPA PALACE...

NEXT DAY... DJEHUTY WAS IN HIS CAMP WHEN THE PRINCE OF JOPPA ARRIVED. BUT BEFORE THEY COULD TALK, A SERVANT RUSHED IN...

SIR, I WAS UNPACKING AND I FOUND THE MAGIC CANE OF TUTHMOSIS IN YOUR LUGGAGE

I'VE HEARD OF THAT MAGIC CANE. I MUST SEE IT

THAT GIVES ME ANOTHER CRAFTY IDEA

MAY I SEE THE MAGIC CANE OF TUTHMOSIS III?

KNEEL IN FRONT OF ME – I'LL HOLD IT OVER YOUR HEAD SO YOU CAN FEEL THE POWER...

AND DJEHUTY SMASHED THE PRINCE ON THE HEAD...

SO? DO YOU FEEL THE POWER?

WHOMP!

UNNNNGGGGG!

47

SERVANT ... TAKE HIS CLOTHES OFF

TWEET TWEET TWEET

THAT'S ALL I SEEM TO DO

DJEHUTY DRESSED IN THE PRINCE'S CLOTHES, THEN RODE TO THE WALLS OF JOPPA.

THE PRINCE WAS BUNDLED INTO A SACK.

WARRIORS OF EGYPT ... CLIMB INTO THESE FIG BASKETS

I'M TOO BIG TO FIT

GREAT NEWS, JOPPANS. I HAVE CAPTURED DJEHUTY

BUT THE EGYPTIAN SOLDIERS IN THE BASKETS JUMPED OUT.

YOU'RE NICKED

I'M TRICKED

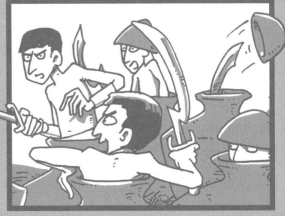

SO I CAPTURED THE MIGHTY CITY AND NO ONE WAS HURT

THE SOLDIERS OF JOPPA WERE TIED UP AND THE PEOPLE TURNED INTO SLAVES.

EXCUSE ME... I THINK YOU ARE FORGETTING THE CANE ON MY BRAIN, AREN'T YOU?

DJEHUTY RETURNED TO EGYPT A HERO - WITH HUNDREDS OF SLAVES.

AND I GET TO KEEP DJEHUTY'S CLOTHES

I REWARD YOU WITH LOTS OF LAND, MY BRAVE GENERAL

50

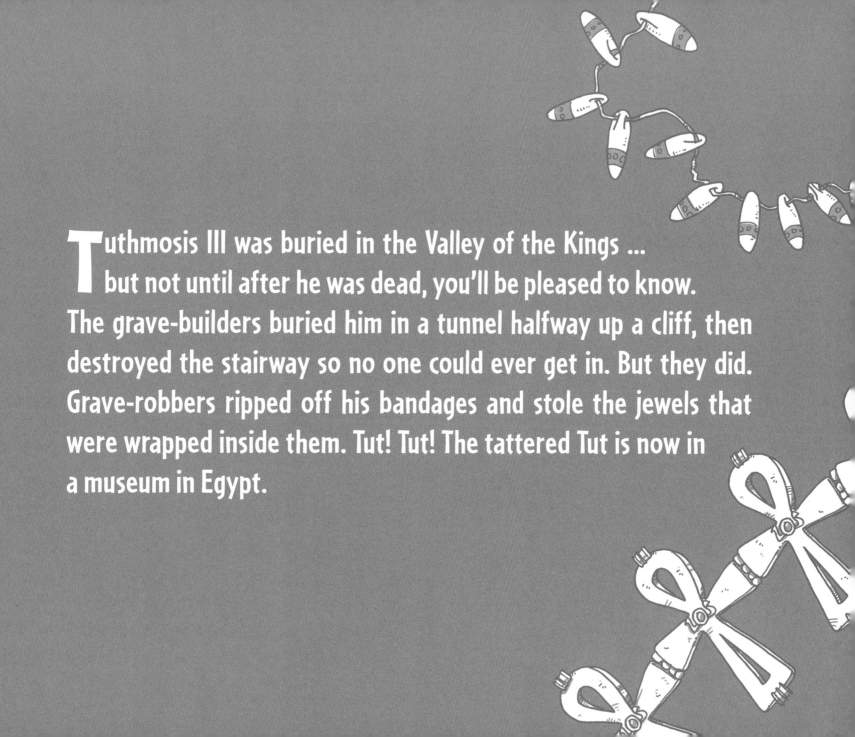

Tuthmosis III was buried in the Valley of the Kings ...
but not until after he was dead, you'll be pleased to know.
The grave-builders buried him in a tunnel halfway up a cliff, then
destroyed the stairway so no one could ever get in. But they did.
Grave-robbers ripped off his bandages and stole the jewels that
were wrapped inside them. Tut! Tut! The tattered Tut is now in
a museum in Egypt.

PEASANT PAIN

AROUND 1500 BC

PARENTS CAN REALLY NAG YOU, CAN'T THEY? WELL, THEY WERE JUST AS BAD THOUSANDS OF YEARS AGO. AN EGYPTIAN DAD, DUA-KHETI, TOLD HIS SON PEPI TO LEARN WRITING - TO BE A 'SCRIBE'. IF THE LAD DIDN'T LEARN HIS LESSONS THEN HE'D END UP WITH A ROTTEN JOB. DUA-KHETI WENT ON TO EXPLAIN JUST HOW PAINFUL IT WAS TO BE A PEASANT.

NOW, PEPI LAD, LET'S HAVE A WALK AROUND AND SEE THE SORT OF MISERABLE LIFE THE POOR PEASANTS LEAD

CAN'T BE AS BAD AS THE MISERABLE LIFE YOU GIVE ME

SEE THE COPPERSMITH AT HIS WORK AT THE DOOR OF HIS FURNACE. HIS FINGERS ARE LIKE THE CLAWS OF THE CROCODILE, AND HE STINKS MORE THAN FISH POO

THAT'S AN INSULT!

AN INSULT TO THE FISH ... PHEW!

THE CARPENTER HERE IS WORN OUT BY HIS WORK. HE EVEN HAS TO WORK BY THE LIGHT OF THE OIL LAMP WHEN THE REST OF US ARE ASLEEP

I COULD GIVE YOU A JOB, PEPI

I WOODEN WANT THAT. HEH! HEH!

I'LL BET THE JEWELLER IS RICH THOUGH?

NOT REALLY. HE HAS TO DRILL OUT THE PRECIOUS STONES THEN STRING THEM TOGETHER

IT MAKES MY POOR BACK ACHE

SENSIBLE PEOPLE WOULD WORK ON A TABLE, NOT ON THE FLOOR

WOOD IS RARE IN EGYPT – PEASANTS CAN'T AFFORD TABLES, YOU MAD LAD

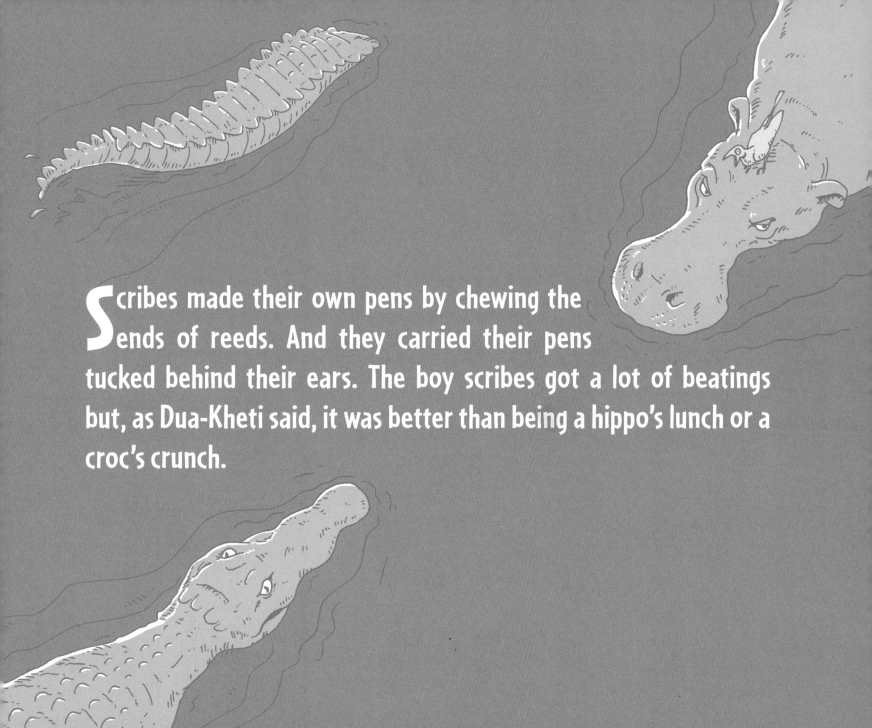

Scribes made their own pens by chewing the ends of reeds. And they carried their pens tucked behind their ears. The boy scribes got a lot of beatings but, as Dua-Kheti said, it was better than being a hippo's lunch or a croc's crunch.

PHARAOH PHIBBER

AROUND 1274 BC

PHARAOH RAMESSES II – RAMESSES THE GREAT – WAS ONE OF THOSE KINGS WHO SPENT ALL HIS LIFE FIGHTING.

HE FOUGHT PIRATES FROM THE SEA, AND WON. HE FOUGHT THE NUBIANS TO THE SOUTH, AND WON. THEN HE FOUGHT THE HITTITES IN THE NORTH AND ... ER ... HE **SAID** HE WON.

BUT ONCE THE EGYPTIANS WERE INSIDE THE CITY, THE HIDDEN HITTITE ARMY APPEARED.

IT'S A TRAP!

RAMESSES FOUGHT HIS WAY OUT OF IT AND MANAGED TO ESCAPE BACK TO EGYPT. HE CALLED THE SCRIBES TO HIS PALACE...

I WANT YOU TO TELL THE STORY OF MY GREAT BATTLE AT KADESH

YOU TELL IT, WE'LL WRITE IT

THE HITTITES ATTACKED. NO OFFICER WAS WITH ME, NO CHARIOT DRIVER, NO EGYPTIAN SOLDIER, NO SHIELD-CARRIER...

YOU FOUGHT THEM SINGLE-HANDED?

AMAZING

THE BIBLE TELLS THIS STORY. BUT THE STORY DOES NOT APPEAR IN ANY EGYPTIAN WRITINGS.

Historians are not sure if the escape of the Hebrew slaves really happened that way. They guess it MAY have been in the time of Ramesses. The great escape is not one of the stories that Ramesses had painted and carved on the monuments of Egypt. But neither is the true story of his 'draw' at Kadesh. Ramesses the great? Or Ramesses the phibbing Pharaoh?

THE **TEN PLAGUES** OF EGYPT

1 WATER → BLOOD

2 FROGS

3 GNATS

4 FLIES

5 PESTILENCE

6 BOILS

7 HAIL

8 LOCUSTS

9 DARKNESS

10 DEATH OF FIRST-BORN CHILD

CRIME TIME

1151 BC

THE PHARAOHS WERE THE RICHEST PEOPLE IN THE WORLD. OF COURSE, LOTS OF PEOPLE MUST HAVE BEEN JEALOUS OF THEM. SOME PEOPLE EVEN PLOTTED TO KILL THE PHARAOH TO GET HIS POWER AND HIS RICHES. IT WAS A DANGEROUS THING TO BE A KING, AS RAMESSES III FOUND OUT. RAMESSES III WAS THE LAST OF THE GREAT EGYPTIAN PHARAOHS ... AND A PALACE PLOT WAS NEARLY THE LAST OF RAMESSES III.

ONE DAY, SON, ALL OF THIS WILL BE YOURS. WHEN RAMESSES IS A MUMMY, OF COURSE

I CAN'T WAIT FOR HIS MUMMY, MUMMY... IN FACT I DON'T SEE WHY I SHOULD WAIT

OF COURSE TIY **DIDN'T** HAVE A LOT OF POWER. BUT SHE AND RAMESSES HAD A SON CALLED PENTEWERE - A FUTURE KING.

SO QUEEN TIY GOT TOGETHER WITH THE TOP PALACE SERVANTS AS WELL AS SIX OTHER WIVES AND SOME IMPORTANT SOLDIERS.

I LOVE RAMESSES SO MUCH, I WOULD LIKE TO SEE HIM HAPPY ... IN THE AFTERLIFE

YEAH. MY MUM WANTS HIM DEAD!

OOOOH!

HOW CAN WE ... ERM ... HELP HIM TO BE HAPPY IN THE AFTERLIFE?

SMASH HIS HEAD IN WHILE HE'S ASLEEP

POISON HIS WINE

I'M PRETTY GOOD AT CUTTING OFF NAUGHTY BITS!

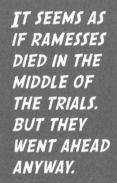

IT SEEMS AS IF RAMESSES DIED IN THE MIDDLE OF THE TRIALS. BUT THEY WENT AHEAD ANYWAY.

HOW DO YOU PLEAD?

HOW DO I PLEAD? I USUALLY GET DOWN ON MY KNEES TO DO IT

I DON'T THINK HE MEANT THAT, MA

YOU WERE THE LEADER OF THE PLOT TO KILL THE PHARAOH, WEREN'T YOU?

TO MAKE ME PHARAOH, MA. DON'T YOU REMEMBER?

WHY WOULD I WANT TO KILL THE GREAT RAMESSES?

QUEEN TIY, YOU HAVE BEEN FOUND GUILTY. I SENTENCE YOU TO DEATH

BETTER LUCK NEXT TIME. I'LL MISS YOU, MA

AND I SENTENCE YOU, PENTEWERE, TO DEATH TOO

WHAT?! ME? YOU CAN'T EXECUTE ME. I'M THE NEXT PHARAOH

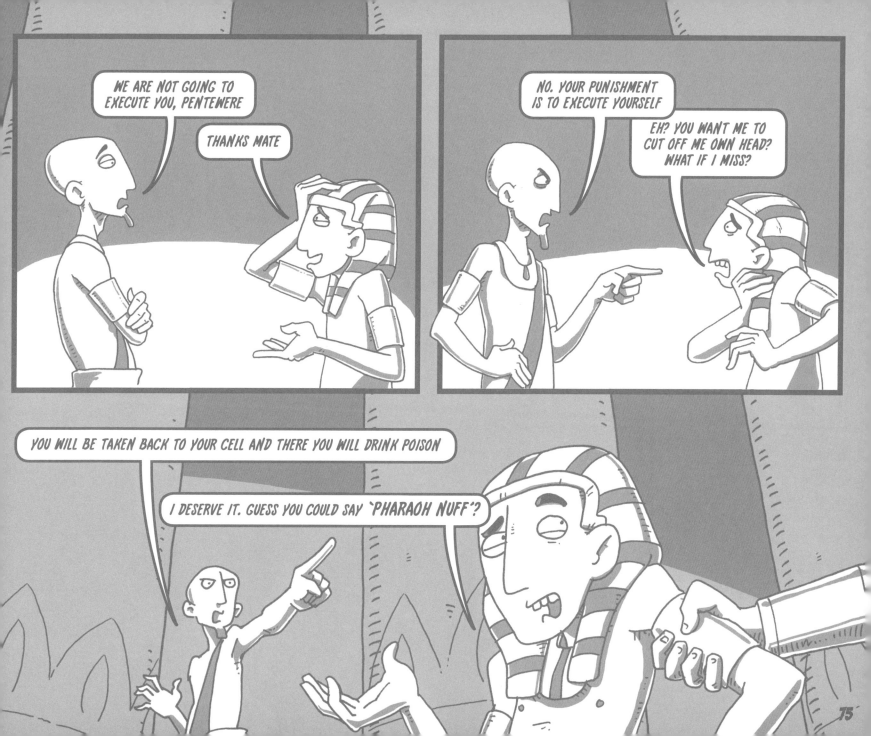

MOST OF THE PLOTTERS WERE FORCED TO DRINK POISON.

CHEERS!

ABOUT 40 PEOPLE WERE EXECUTED. SOME OF THE JUDGES TOOK MONEY TO LET THEIR FRIENDS GO FREE. THE JUDGES WERE CAUGHT.

YOUR PUNISHMENT IS TO HAVE YOUR NOSE AND YOUR EARS CUT OFF

HOW WILL I SMELL?

AS BAD AS EVER

Ramesses III was the last of the great Pharaohs. After him Egypt struggled with attacks from outside the country and rebels inside. Ramesses III died and the great days of Egypt died with him. Nothing lasts forever.

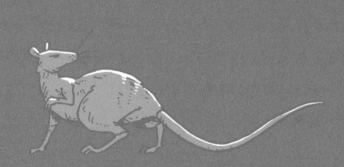

CLEOPATRA, THE LAST QUEEN

30 BC

THE GREAT DAYS OF ANCIENT EGYPT WERE OVER. THE COUNTRY WAS RULED BY GREEKS, BUT THE REALLY POWERFUL PEOPLE IN THE WORLD WERE THE ROMANS. GREEK QUEEN CLEOPATRA RULED EGYPT. WHAT A ROTTEN RULER.

CLEO WAS NOT BEAUTIFUL. HISTORIANS SAY SHE HAD A LONG HOOKED NOSE, A THICK NECK AND LOOKED MORE LIKE A MAN.

BUT THE BOYS ALL LOVE ME TO BITS. WHY?

WHO NOSE?

CLEO WAS REALLY CLEVER. SHE SPOKE NINE LANGUAGES...

BUT NOT ALL AT THE SAME TIME

PTOLEMY THE THIRTEENTH ... LUCKY FOR SOME

BUT UNLUCKY FOR PTOLEMY — HE DROWNED IN THE NILE

SOME SAY CLEO PUSHED HIM...

NO I DIDN'T

THAT'S A DENIAL

NO ... IT'S DA NILE

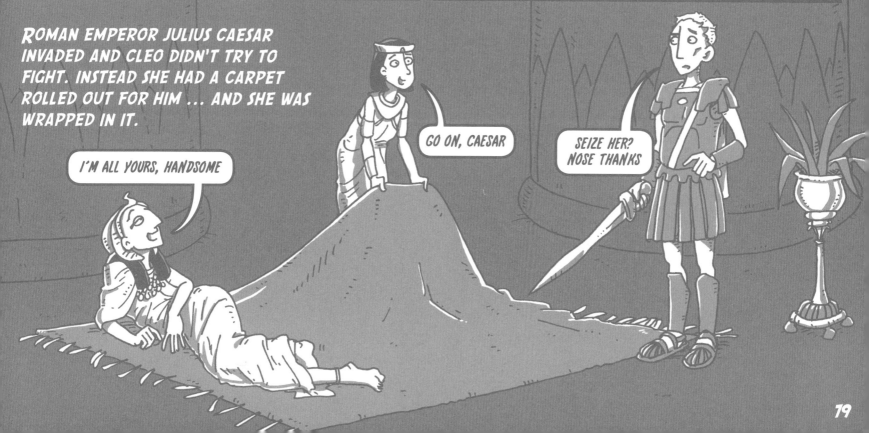

ROMAN EMPEROR JULIUS CAESAR INVADED AND CLEO DIDN'T TRY TO FIGHT. INSTEAD SHE HAD A CARPET ROLLED OUT FOR HIM ... AND SHE WAS WRAPPED IN IT.

I'M ALL YOURS, HANDSOME

GO ON, CAESAR

SEIZE HER? NOSE THANKS

MARK ANTONY STABBED HIMSELF IN THE STOMACH BUT MADE A MESS OF IT AND DIDN'T DIE QUICKLY.

OH I WILL NEVER JOIN MY DEAR DEAD CLEO

SHE ISN'T DEAD, ANT. IT WAS JUST A LIE

WHEN MARK ANTONY HEARD THE TRUTH HE ASKED TO BE CARRIED TO HER.

I AM DYING, CLEO, DYING

THIS MAN HAS GUTS

I KNOW AND THEY'RE SPILLING OUT ONTO THE FLOOR

MARK ANTONY DIED. CLEO WAS CAPTURED BY THE ROMAN EMPEROR OCTAVIAN.

I'M A CLEO-CAPTURER. I'LL PARADE HER THROUGH THE STREETS LIKE A COMMON CRIMINAL

I'D RATHER DIE

WHAT HAPPENED NEXT? DEPENDS WHO YOU BELIEVE. TEACHERS SAY...

SNAKE ARM

CLEOPATRA SMUGGLED A POISONOUS SNAKE INTO HER PRISON AND LET IT BITE HER ON THE ARM

BUT THE HORRIBLE HISTORIES TALE SAYS SHE WAS MURDERED. OCTAVIAN TOLD HER SERVING GIRLS...

KILL YOUR MISTRESS ... OR DIE

HAPPY TO HELP, OCCY

I'VE NEVER KILLED ANYONE BEFORE – BUT I'M HAPPY TO HAVE A STAB AT IT

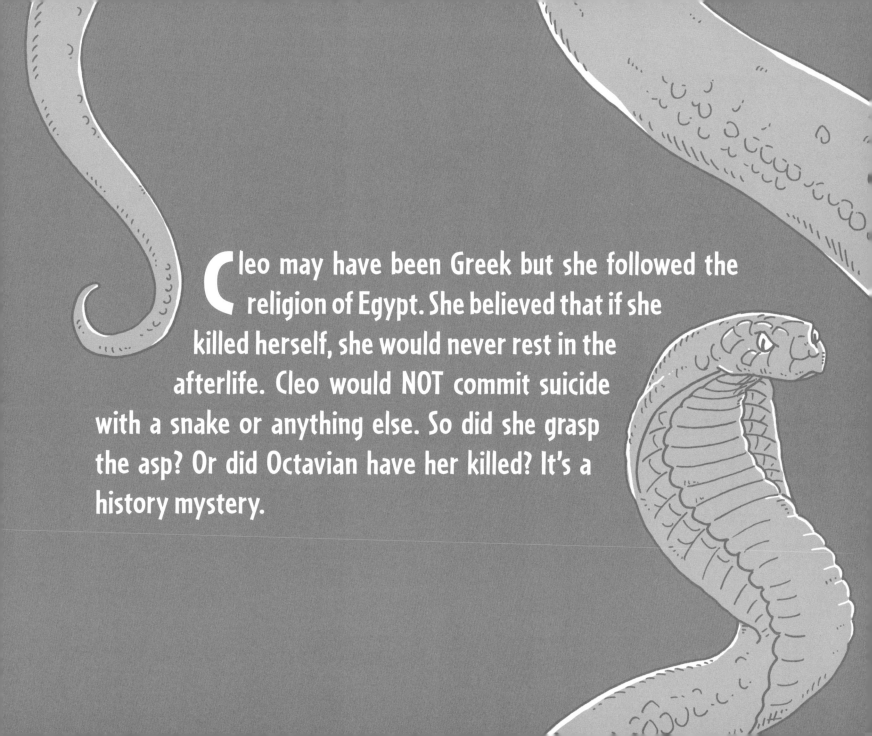

Cleo may have been Greek but she followed the religion of Egypt. She believed that if she killed herself, she would never rest in the afterlife. Cleo would NOT commit suicide with a snake or anything else. So did she grasp the asp? Or did Octavian have her killed? It's a history mystery.

CRAZY CURSES

1890

THE IDEA OF MAKING MUMMIES STARTED WITH THE STRANGE STORY OF OSIRIS. AND IT ENDS WITH THE STRANGE STORY OF A MUMMY CURSE. SOME PEOPLE BELIEVE THAT IF YOU DISTURB A MUMMY'S GRAVE YOU WILL MEET A HORRIBLE HEND ... I MEAN 'END'. THE STORY IS AS TRUE AS THE TALE OF AMEN-RA...

IN THE 1880S, FOUR EGYPTIAN ROBBERS DUG UP A MUMMY AND TOOK IT AWAY TO SELL...

I WILL GIVE YOU THREE YOUR SHARE OF THE MONEY AND I'LL KEEP THE MUMMY. I TAKE THE RISK THAT IT MAY BE WORTHLESS

SOUNDS FAIR ENOUGH

THE ROBBER TOOK IT TO HIS HOTEL ROOM. BUT ONE NIGHT HE SAID...

I AM GOING FOR A WALK!

HE WALKED INTO THE DESERT AND WAS NEVER SEEN AGAIN.

CURSE HIM! HEH! HEH!

THE SECOND ROBBER TOOK THE MUMMY HOME. BUT HE ARGUED WITH A SERVANT.

THAT MUMMY WILL BRING BAD LUCK!

THEN GET OUT. YOU ARE SACKED

THE SERVANT DREW A GUN AND SHOT THE ROBBER IN THE ARM.

BANG

AAAAGGGGH!

IN LIFE SHE WAS THE PRIESTESS, AMEN-RA. A WICKED WOMAN

SHE DIED IN 1500 BC

SHE HAD A HUNDRED PEOPLE SOLD AS SLAVES OR TORTURED TO DEATH

THEN ONE OF HER LOVERS STABBED HER TO DEATH

OH DEAR. THAT WAS A BIT DAFT.
I CAN'T DO ANY MORE CURSING. CURSES!

There are many such stories of curses. Old mummies bringing death and misery to the modern world. Are they true? Make up your own mind.

LOOK OUT
FOR
TUDORS
A HIGH-SPEED HISTORY

TERRY DEARY

ILLUSTRATED BY
DAVE SMITH